From The Front Desk To The Corner Office

Maria Stanfield

From The Front Desk To The Corner Office

Copyright © 2018 by Maria Stanfield

All rights reserved. No part of this work may be reproduced, transmitted, stored in any form whatsoever, printed, electronic download, photocopying, recording by any information storage and retrieval system, or individual without the prior written permission of the author.

ISBN 978-1983725678

Published by Maria Stanfield
Website: www.mysisterceo.com
Email: maria@mysisterceo.com

Published by Regina Robinson Enterprises
www.reginarobinsonspeaks.com

Acknowledgement

Writing this book in many ways was like having a baby. I was pregnant with the idea for a long time. When sharing the news with my family and friends they showered me with encouragement throughout the birthing process.

My Doctors (Family)

To my mom and my best friend, Mary Coates, thank you for believing in me since birth. You have always been my rock and my Shero.

Heartfelt hugs to my beautiful daughters, who bring me so much joy and are my greatest reward. You are my everything. Thank you for always loving and encouraging me.

To Kevin, my love and greatest supporter. God knew exactly what I needed when he sent you into my life and I am so grateful for you. Thank you for telling me to "go for it" and having my back throughout the process. While I was at work climbing the corporate ladder of my career you were the glue that held our family together. You went to every game and event, cooked dinner and read bedtime stories to the kids. I was only able to play big at work because you were playing big at home and for that I am forever grateful. This book is not about my success it's about our success as a family. Thank you for your prayers, support, guidance and tough love.

The Godmothers

Thank you Rosita Banks-Taylor, Regina Parks, Darlene DeMoss, My SOBA sisters, Jaunita Banks, Karen Que, Nicole Clough, Kenia Garner, Donna Stewart, Brenda McCain and all of my incredible sistersfriends who have always remained close and stood by me through thick and thin. Thank you for supporting me in writing and publishing my first book.

My Lamaze Coaches

Thank you Kathy Kelly, Chris Kinchen, Jeanine Elgin, Doreen Rainey, Nicole Roberts Jones, and Janice Lowery for teaching me how to breathe through the process. You BOSS women led by example and taught me to be a feminine and fierce leader in my career, business and life. I wouldn't be here without you ladies.

The Midwives

Thank you to the women who joined me in the delivery room. The faithful few who were brave enough to join me in the laboring of getting this book pushed out.

Ayisha Hayes was the first one I told the news that I was "expecting" to write a book and needed help. She along with storyteller Stephanie Parrot walked me through the first two trimesters of this journey to help me find the right words to express my story. Through the process we became sisters. You two are amazing!

Kim Ross thanks for checking the fingers and toes, as you scrupulously read through my first draft with a fine tooth comb.

A Special Thanks to **Regina Robinson** - My birthing coach. Regina thank you for being in my ear, encouraging me to push when I was tired, confused or whenever I started to shrink back. After many hours of labor, you were there to catch the baby, clean her up (editing) and hand me my beautiful masterpiece "From The Front Desk To The Corner Office!"

To every person who is pregnant with a story, I encourage you now is the time to *Deliver*!

Testimonials

With a Christ-centered focus, My Sisters Closet and My Sister CEO empowers women to reach their full potential by providing opportunities for professional, spiritual and economic transformation. My Sisters Closet and My Sister CEO develops confident women leaders who, in turn, become an inspiration to other women – creating a cycle of success. These organizations are truly impactful and life-changing.

—Nita Banks

I am so excited for Maria and proud of her decision to write this book. Having known her for several years now, it's clear that Maria has a message to share and there is an audience that needs to hear it! You may ask "What makes Maria different from so many others offering the skills and expertise to help people be their best?" The best answer is that she actually practices what she "preaches!" Maria is not only dedicated to her family but also active in her church and community. With her magnetic personality and infectious energy, she has effectively navigated professional waters to climb the ladder to success, while maintaining a healthy work-life balance. Her thirty years+ of working in talent acquisition, performance management, leadership and talent development has given her keen insight on the best practices to find success in her career journey. If you want a leg up on the competition, getting this book is a must!

—Rosita Banks-Taylor

My Sister CEO is a powerful community of businesswomen who give true meaning to, "I Am Your Sister Not Your Competition." As an emerging entrepreneur, my connection to My Sister CEO allows me access to business strategies, coaching, mentorship, and the strength of an authentic sisterhood of sisters helping sisters. Maria Stanfield is the example of her professional expertise, business genius and her drive to thrive that makes My Sister CEO breed success stories.

—Nicole Clough, Entrepreneur
Crowned To Love Rhinestone Apparel

Maria is a beacon for sisterhood at it's best, meeting people where they are and helping them rise to shine their light brighter whether she's in neglected community neighborhoods, in the boardroom, or somewhere in between. Her work is making a lasting impact, touching so many as a coach, mentor, community leader, CEO, mom, wife, and child of God. She sows hope, joy, and faith into every aspect of life, leading by example with ease and grace. The best part is that this is just the beginning of a powerful legacy in the making.

—Karen Que, CEO/Founder

I Am My Sister's Keeper

I am writing this book for the woman who feels like she is alone, not good enough or not qualified. This book is for the woman who has been told she doesn't have the experience and knowledge necessary to walk in her greatness. In the Bible, the Book of Psalms 119:105 reads, "Your word is a lamp unto my feet and a light to my path." God's word clearly tells us that our path is set before us and He is our guide. God reminded me that my journey prepared me for so much more than I could have ever imagined. And to think I was compiling a binder of my career experiences and accomplishments in order to obtain a college degree society deems as my ticket to the top. God opened doors that I once thought could only be opened with a piece of paper!

A defining moment in my career called for me to submit a 600-page delineation experiential learning proposal that would allow me to earn college credits for my work experience. The report outlined twelve subject areas within my career journey; along with the knowledge and experiential learning I received in these categories. While I worked diligently to write out my experiential learning document, my coworkers were amazing and supported me to ensure all of my work was taken care of and that my duties were fulfilled. Never underestimate the support of your team. In the final week prior to submission deadline, I remained focused and determined with every stroke of the keyboard, so much so that my husband would leave home for the day and return reminding me; "Maria you are in the same spot! Have you even eaten?" I was so determined to complete the mission and knowing that I had a group of supporters not only at home backing me, but also at work eased my worries. Having my eight colleagues from top leadership, supervisory and administrative staff all willing to take a portion of the document outlining a subject area working diligently to review my life's professional work. The women got together and supported me through proofreading, editing and anything needed to ensure I had a finished product by the deadline. They reminded me of the women across the span of my career who have helped to pull me along in my journey. I was reminded as I stood side-by-side the power of Sisterhood. In the end, I had a binder that encompassed my entire career earning me twenty-eight college credits out of the thirty. My credentials nor my educational background mattered to my colleagues they were just there to support me and see me succeed.

The world we live in has a way of making you feel like you're not qualified if you don't have a college degree. Today, I realize my journey *From The Front Desk To The Corner Office* never had anything to do with obtaining a degree. Instead, it had all to do with a sisterhood of mentors, faith and the tenacity to never give up on my dreams. What I realized was the very thing I had been hiding from I already had within. I believe that where you find void or lack, that is the very area God wants you to lean on Him.

I am a living testimony that if you are willing to walk by faith and not by sight, you can achieve anything you set out to accomplish. As you read my book I pray that you can see yourself within the pages and that my struggles and experiences will give you the strength and courage to take one step at a time. Knowing you have a Sister CEO who supports you. In fact, you have an entire community of powerful, empowered women, whose ultimate goal is to encourage one another daily as a reminder that we can accomplish all things. My desire is that any area you feel is lacking, I pray the words shared in this book will shift your perspective to a life of abundance.

Where The Story Begins

Growing up as a thin six feet tall woman my career aspirations were to become a fashion model. With countless auditions, low paying modeling jobs, and a few TV appearances, I quickly realized I needed a career that paid well or a rich husband. I know you're wondering, which one came first. Let's just say after working several retail and restaurant jobs, I finally landed a corporate position at a law firm as a receptionist. Now just in case you lost hope I married my not so rich prince charming that same year. It marked a pivotal milestone in my life as a twenty-five year-old woman struggling to find my true purpose, yet lacking the confidence to believe in myself. Despite the challenges during this season of my life it turned out to be the beginning of an amazing journey. It's not over yet! I still have so many things I plan to accomplish.

The most rewarding part of my life is being present to witness the results of my continuous efforts to make an impact professionally and personally. It truly warms my heart to hear women and men share how I gave them a second chance when no one else would support them in changing their lives and igniting their careers. It is pure joy and humbling to know the gift of mentorship that was bestowed upon me by many powerhouse women in leadership I am now able to mentor others.

The directness from my mentors taught me how to hone in on my skills of being a master interviewer. One story that stands out to me is a woman whom I had the opportunity to interview. Recently our paths crossed, she ran up and hugged me tight saying how I changed her life during our interview. She said,

> I would never forget the question you asked me, "What is that thing that makes your heart skip a beat?" She said that question touched my heart and pushed me to examine myself from within.

I didn't remember her, but she remembered me. You never know whose life you will touch and leave an impact. What keeps me going is the inspiration and encouragement from my family and the women whose lives I have had an opportunity to impact.

Family First

As my husband and I drove home from the hospital after the birth of my first baby girl Miranda, I stared at her sweet beautiful face and cried uncontrollably. My husband looked back and nervously asked,

"What's wrong, do you need me to pull over?"
Still sobbing, I asked him, "How are we going to care for this baby?" We were barely managing our own lives; we were in over our heads in debt because of poor financial decisions we had made. To put it mildly our finances were a wreck. And the reality of caring for another human being was overwhelming. Kevin's response still rings in my head today,

"We are going to pray and ask God to help us."
In the backseat of the car I laid hands on our little girl and prayed over her. I committed her to God and asked Him to take care of her. I promised God that we would raise her to know and love him. I prayed the same prayer after the birth of my next two daughters, Roberta and Dominique.

My life is filled with happiness and five very special people keep my heart fluently beating every day. They are truly my number one supporters. It is truly amazing to travel this journey with a man who truly loves and adores me. The day he made me his wife we vowed to cover one another till death do us part and he does just that. Recently, my husband and I attended a Valentine's Day brunch where the husbands were instructed to take their wives hands and pray over them. My husband began to pray and declare over my life how proud he was that selflessly, I was harnessing in on my gift to personally and spiritually change the world, one person at a time. That was a special moment I will never forget. He truly is a man who covers not just me, but also our beautiful daughters and granddaughter. I know that every step I take my three daughters and granddaughter are watching. Therefore I ensure my steps are carefully traced.

Each one of my daughters hold a very special place in my heart. They are very protective of me and I so love them for that.

In 1988, after five years of trying to conceive, we were told it wasn't meant to be, but God decided differently. He blessed us with my oldest daughter Miranda (affectionately referred to as my twin). She gave the greatest gift any mother could ask for, a beautiful granddaughter. While in the hospital giving birth to our precious princess, my daughter looked up at me and said, "That woman right there, that is a praying woman. I hear her in the morning crying and praying for her family." In the midst of experiencing labor and on medication she remembered the most important thing the power of prayer. That touched me deeply, I couldn't have asked for a better blessing in that moment. I felt as if right there I was passing the baton of prayer to my daughter so that in return she can share it with her baby girl.

My middle daughter Roberta is full of grace and intelligence. Roberta pushes me to thrive. She is a business mogul. I can always depend on her to support me in solving problems within my business. She touched my heart recently when she bought us a beautiful mother/daughter journal. Regularly we write in the journal passing it back and forth as we recorded the things we remember and our experiences together. One of the entries Roberta wrote about was how she appreciates how I love her and allow her to be herself. The moments we share in our journal will forever be a blessing.

Growing up my youngest daughter, Dominique was never far behind. Whenever you would see me you would see Dominique. From the time she was a little girl she would always grace us through dance. It became her first love. When it was time for her to apply to college she chose performing arts schools. Her first choice school placed her on the waitlist. You can imagine she was devastated. Other schools accepted and offered her a scholarship, but she wanted to wait for her first choice. I reminded her that she'd have to make a decision. She shared that in her prayer time with God, He told her to wait and confirmed it through the song "Wait on the Lord," by Fred Hammond. I stood in agreement with my baby and we waited. The next day she called me screaming, her first choice school removed her from the waitlist. She was in! She taught me in that moment that what God has for you, is for you, if you stand in faith. She said I taught her but the truth of the matter, she had more faith than her mother. Know matter how high I climb, my greatest reward is the love and support I have from my family!

Forever Grateful

Today, while employed as a law firm Administrator, I also run a non-profit, My Sisters Closet and a coaching practice. Everyday I am thankful for blessings I could have never imagined; working from a large corner office and earning a salary that allows my family to live a comfortable life. I come from a praying family that believes that God can do exceedingly, abundantly, above all. Once I came to the realization that the blessings included me, my life was transformed.

Table Of Contents

Acknowledgement 3

Testimonial Page 6

I Am My Sister's Keeper 9

Where The Story Begins 13

Family First 15

Forever Grateful 19

Step 1: **S** – Serve Others 23

Step 2: **U** – Understand Your Full Potential 33

Step 3: **C** – Challenge Yourself To Do More 51

Step 4: **C** – Commit To YOU 61

Step 5: **E** – Elevate Your Mindset 71

Step 6: **S** – Stand In Your Confidence 79

Step 7: **S** – Stay Relevant 89

The Best Is Yet To Come 97

Get To Know Maria 98

My Sister CEO 100

Step 1

1
Serve Others

One of the ultimate models of service is Jesus. He was all about serving the people. The type of love and service Jesus shared has surrounded me my entire life. From my great grandmothers, my parents and my family, serving and supporting others was a lifestyle everyone demonstrated daily.

Growing up, my grandmother would collect shoeboxes and fill them up with personal items like toothbrushes, toothpaste, and toiletries. She didn't stop there. She would knit gloves and hats and add them in the shoeboxes and pass them out to people on the streets. Also, when we would go to church she would serve in the kitchen making sandwiches for those in need. I can remember as a young girl helping her, so being of service to others is just something I have always seen as a normal way of life. It is no surprise that today I run My Sisters Closet! Being of service is deeply rooted in my DNA. I don't think twice about being of service to someone else, professionally or personally.

In my journey, I have lived by the words of the late Maya Angelou, "When you learn, teach. When you get, give." My focus has been how can I be of support to others and not how they can benefit me. My life agenda is to simply ask if I can help.

My first corporate job working as a receptionist, I found myself with a lot of downtime. I noticed the Director of HR was always so busy. She would arrive early and regularly work late into the evening. After a short time of being at the firm and observing her process, I asked if there was anything I could do to assist her. She declined my offer. However, recommended I ask her assistants if there was anything I could do to help lighten their workload. Now some people might take that as a rejection; however, I saw it as a golden opportunity. I wasn't working directly with the HR Director, but she gave me an open door to work closely with her team. I reached out to her assistants immediately and of course they accepted my help. They immediately gave me tasks to assist with such projects as, providing and retrieving applicant paperwork and logging non-confidential information into a spreadsheet. Now in the eyes of some this may seem like tedious tasks but to me it was my opportunity to enter their space and learn new skills. My willingness to serve paid off earning me a position in the HR department just a few years later. This is just one example of the many service-oriented tasks that helped me climb the corporate ladder to success. Reflecting back, I know that if I had not asked if I could help, I probably would have stayed at that receptionist desk a lot longer.

Serving other people should start from the inside out and not the outside in. What I mean by this is, having a heart to help and serve others because you know it's the right thing to do. The gift of service is a wonderful gift. However, I have learned from experience that it's all about yielding to the Holy Spirit when it comes to how and when to serve others. Even though you may have good intentions in serving someone, the reality is you may not be serving that person the way they need to be served.

I used to love McDonald's hot vanilla lattes. So much so, I often stopped to get one every morning. That was a moment of confession on my part. Don't hold it against me. While in line one morning, I heard about a challenge called the Drive-thru Difference, where you go through the drive-thru, pay for your meal and the person's meal behind you. You then ask the cashier for the receipt of the person behind you and write on it "Jesus loves you", or "God's thinking of you," whatever you want to write, then give the receipt back to the cashier to give to them and drive off. I always tried to make sure I was gone before they have a chance to stop and thank me, because that's not what it's about. It's not about me. In fact it was a way for me to serve others and show God's love. I'll admit, I often looked in my rear view mirror not for celebration, but to see the excitement in the people's faces that someone decided to bless them.

One day, the drive-thru line was extremely long so I parked and went inside. I saw a couple with a baby in line who looked as if they had possibly fallen on hard times and were struggling to pay. I was behind them so I told the cashier I would pay for their order. At that moment the man got so upset with me. "No you will not!" He yelled. He proceeded to express his disdain. His wife stood there holding the baby trying to tell her husband they needed the help. She recognized I was only trying to help. At this point, I just left realizing even though what I was doing was out of the kindness of my heart; I was reminded that this might be a time where I was serving what he didn't need at that time. Not to mention, I felt this wasn't a situation the Holy Spirit had nudged me to intervene in. In fact, I made the decision to be of service on my own. "God knows our hearts." And in this situation, He not only knew my heart He knew the man's heart, which is probably why He didn't impress upon me to be of service to him. Surely this family needed help; however, I was not assigned to help them nor did I know the way they needed to be helped at that time. This was a reminder to always seek the Holy Spirit for guidance on whom I should serve and in what capacity.

Interestingly, a few weeks later I was driving down the street and for some reason I was running a little late (I don't like to be late). I notice a woman walking down the street and I hear the Lord say, "pick her up." Now, normally I'm not one to question God but the human side of me kicked in and I got a little nervous about what He was commanding me to do. I continued driving down the street, talking out loud to God and asking Him, "Are you sure? What if she tries to hurt me? What if she doesn't want to get in the car?" To which He responds, "Would I tell you to do something that's going to hurt you?" Now you may wonder, "Maria, how in the world did you know this was God and not just you deciding to help someone that doesn't want to be helped again?" After the last incident when I moved on my own, I learned to ask the Lord this simple question: "God is this You or me?" I don't know how to explain it but I get a physical vibration in my chest. What I call my "Knower." If I don't get that alert from my "Knower" I don't proceed. This time, it was confirmed. I knew I had to be obedient, so I let out a heavy sigh (in agreement of course) and agreed. By this time, I had already passed the woman so I made a u-turn, went back, pulled up beside her, rolled down my window and said, "The Lord told me to pick you up." Right then, it began to rain and not just a sprinkle. It was those pelting drops of rain that sounded like they were being thrown with force. Without hesitation the woman says, "okay" and she hopped in the car. That's how I knew it was God because any other time, someone may have thought I was crazy by pulling up and telling them the Lord told me to pick them up!

As I drove down the street, I started making small talk with the woman but thinking inside my head that I'm going to be late to my destination. Can you believe it? Her destination was right across the street from mine? Not only did the Lord put me in a position to be of service to someone who needed it, He also allowed me to fulfill my responsibility of being on time to my destination. That's just how He works! That day in McDonald's, I was acting out of impulse and trying to help someone based off of what I thought they needed. An assumption I made from looking at them, which was wrong. Had I listened to the Holy Spirit, I probably would have known that attempting to serve this family wasn't the right thing to do, at least not in the way I was trying to serve them.

I know that serving others can be a true benefit to the person if they are seeking help. I now know that serving is about being available and willing to do what is asked of you. If you're willing to ask if you can help someone, be willing to do whatever is needed. In some instances you may feel uncomfortable asking at first, but I truly believe the ones that don't yield the results you are expecting, will be a blessing to the person you are serving. I can remember hearing someone say, "Your blessing is often on the other side of you being a blessing to someone else." I believe that is true. The law of reaping and sowing is real; God established it from the beginning of time. We reap what we sow, good and bad. Having a servant heart makes for an abundance of overflow.

Having a service mentality will benefit you as you climb the ladder to success. If you look at all that's going on in the world today, there are many opportunities to be of service. Let's take the natural disasters we have had lately as an example. While we were sitting at home watching the damage that occurred as a result of these disasters, our first reaction was "I want to help!" Which is an amazing thing. However, because we are not there in the thick of the disaster area, we often lack insight on how to help and be of service effectively. During the natural disaster, Hurricane Harvey I remember seeing on television that the city officials were begging people not to send anymore clothes because they had no where to put them. Of course it was a nice gesture but the need for clothing had been met. However, they were in dire need of diapers, baby formula, and other toiletries. The point I want to drive is that it's all about finding out how you can serve others versus assuming what their needs are. In these cases you have to go the extra mile and do some research to find out what's needed.

Being of service to others, while it is the right thing to do, can also have a flip side to it. People who know that you have a heart for serving others may attempt to take advantage of your kindness or, as the cliché states, "take your kindness for weakness." However, we must not live our lives reluctant to serve, because we believe people will use us. Instead we must use discernment and not be afraid to respectfully tell them "no" by any means. In a professional environment, you can usually spot when this is happening because those people will always have something they need help with, pass on their workload to you and all of a sudden magically have an abundance of free time. In your personal life, this may be harder to identify and even harder to say "no" to. You just have to use your best judgment. Seek God for His wisdom if you feel as though whatever is being asked is not in alignment with your values. It's ok to simply say "No."

By now you have a clearer understanding of what it means to serve others so I leave you with this question, what's your next ask?

_____

_____

_____

_____

_____

_____

_____

Take a minute to think about how you can be of service to the people around you, whether at work or in your personal life?

_____

_____

_____

_____

_____

_____

_____

At work, how can you be of service in a way that helps someone individually as well as make a positive difference for your organization overall?

_____

_____

_____

_____

_____

_____

Maybe you have a colleague you know who is having a hard time. I have had days where one of my peers has done something as simple as bring me a cup of coffee. Some might view that as small. However, at the time it honestly made my day. Not because I was dying for caffeine, it was just the thought that someone cared enough to consider me. You never know who has their eyes on you in the workplace. From the higher-ups to those who work under you, never become closed off to being of service if the opportunity presents itself. Someone is always paying attention. And I assure you that the act of sowing and reaping does pay off!

In your personal life, has God been telling you to do something to help another person but you're afraid?

How do you discern the voice of God?

Step 2

Understand Your Potential

2
Understand Your Potential

I have always admired others doing amazing things while I sat on the sidelines. It wasn't until I linked arms with a community of fierce businesswomen who live unapologetically that I started walking in my full potential. Being a part of this sister circle yields accountability, encouragement and mentorship among women who talk the talk and walk the walk. Watching so many talented women of various facets ignited my passion to expand my life's vision.

Whether it's a corporate job or entrepreneurship you must take a visionary approach. Think about the direction you want to take in your life, career, finances, etc. Plan with imagination and take the action that will move you closer to your dream. Know that everything you need is in you and/or around you for your success.

With every step you climb up the corporate ladder, it is necessary to up-level your mindset. Meaning you have to magnify your thinking beyond the current status quo. I want to share two key power plays that worked for me early in my career and business: dressing for success and the power of networking.

Dress For Success

I will never forget my first day as a Human Resources Assistant for a top law firm. After working as the front desk receptionist for years, the time had finally come. I was about to make my debut as a member of the HR Department. This was an entry-level position into the career I had dreamed about since joining the firm. All I could think about was it was going to be a great day. I was getting dressed for my big day, putting the final touches to my outfit. I walked out of the bedroom, cute and confident in my stylish ensemble. As soon as I stepped into his line of vision, my husband looked me up and down and said,

"Where do you think you're going?"

I had no idea what he meant. Surely he remembered that today was my first day in HR. We had just talked about it less than twelve hours ago. Maybe he forgot? I responded, "Where do you think I'm going? I'm going to work." As soon as I said that, my husband raised an eyebrow as if to say, "Oh, really?" I stood there confused with an attitude that was not so pretty. With a loving, heavy sigh, the kind that you get from someone who loves you and is pained because they realize they are about to shatter some form of your faulty perception. He took the time to explain to me where he was coming from. He siad,

> "When you walk into a meeting with what you are wearing, I want you to understand what I see from a man's perspective, I see form-fitting attire on an attractive woman, which sends the message of sexuality. Is that what you want the men in the room to envision when they see you? They will hear little

of what you are saying because they are imagining things that do not relate to work or professionalism. Do you want to be taken seriously, as a professional or is this how you want them to connect with you?"

Right away, my feelings were hurt and I was instantly annoyed…I replied no. I was angry because I thought I looked great! However, he shared a perspective I didn't have: a man's viewpoint.

If I didn't know anything else, I knew fashion! I had a modeling career and my clothes were always fashion forward. I realized that I was so focused on wearing the up-to-date trendy fashion that I neglected to pay close attention to professional appropriateness of my attire. I angrily spun around on my four-inch heels to walk back into the bedroom and change into a suit that was better suited for the corporate office setting. I wanted so bad to believe I had made a smart decision in my initial outfit selection, but the reality was my husband was right. While it hurt to hear what he said, I knew he had a point. As a professional himself in Corporate America he has witnessed the tragic, career-ending results a wrong impression can implant. Knowing he has been privy to private leadership discussions behind closed doors in the boardroom, I was thankful to have his guidance and perspective. In fact, it shifted my thinking because the words came from someone I *knew* had my best interest at heart. On that day my loving husband helped me up-level my mindset. Which in return played a significant role in elevating my career. From that day forward, I asked myself every morning before getting dressed, "What message do I want to send with my attire?" I have always been one to make sure I owned my personality through my wardrobe and I wanted to continue to do that.

Most importantly, my goals were to send a message of professionalism, to receive respect and to make sure I was dressed for the job I wanted and not the job I had. Don't get me wrong, I was grateful for my position; however, it was not where I planned to stay. It was a stepping-stone to my dream career and I showed up daily dressed for the part. I remember my law firm, which was very conservative, transitioned to casual Fridays. I loved wearing my jeans to work on Friday's until I noticed that no one in leadership was wearing jeans. Why? They were the bosses and jeans did not signify upper-level leadership. I knew my ultimate goal was to one day take on a leadership role, so I dressed for the part, at *all* times. Some may think that's old school thinking but it worked for them and it worked for me. Today, I am the Director of Administration for a AMLAW 100 law firm. When anyone walks into our office, client, applicant or guest, and they see me walking through the lobby, they know I'm the boss without me saying a word. Keep this in mind as you continue to grow throughout your career. I know it's cliché but, "dressing for the job you want," has always been and will always be a crucial key to success.

People make assumptions about who you are for themselves based on their initial impression of you. That initial impression is usually based on ones outward physical appearance. I want to share some tips with you on how to ensure your wardrobe aligns with where you want to go and on an affordable budget. While looking the part in the workplace is definitely a necessity, it can also be quite costly. As I mentioned prior, I came from a professional modeling background. Most of my wardrobe was, what I like to call, "couture casual." When I entered corporate America, I did not own any professional attire whatsoever and I didn't really have the means of purchasing a brand new wardrobe at the time. Not to mention, once I had children, adding to my professional attire became even more difficult. Therefore, I pulled it together in the most cost effective way I knew how; I shopped at thrift stores and yard sales. As a matter of fact, the first five to eight years of my career, my wardrobe came from yard sales and thrift stores. I remember times while shopping at yard sales I would find some beautiful suits. And when the women would see me shopping for myself as well as for my kids, they would always give me more. I would ask for the price on one suit and they would give me two. Their kindness was a showcase of sisters linking arms to help one another. In fact, their generosity was part of my inspiration to start my non-profit organization, "My Sisters Closet." My Sisters Closet is an organization that goes out into the community to serve women of all backgrounds. We help women with everything from resume and interview skills to providing them with free, professional attire for their jobs and interviews. We are able to serve the women because of donations from women within the community. We provide them with one suit initially and if they get the job we supply them with a week's worth of clothing.

    Don't be afraid to ask for a helping hand when first starting out. Remember, don't believe what you see on television of how people are living lavish lives all while wearing the latest designer clothes. You can absolutely look professional on a tight budget. Here are a few secret tips on how to *Up-level your Closet on a Budget:*

- *Closet Swap and Consignment* – My girlfriends and I love to shop and save! Try hosting a party of women in your general size. Invite them to bring clothes, jewelry and handbags. Organize the items in one room, refreshments in another and your guests can shop to grab items based on the number of tickets. All leftover items can be donated. Consignment shopping for high-end designer items is the way to go! There are apps such as **Tradesy** where you can sell and buy top designer items for a fraction of the cost. It's all about saving!

- *Outlet shopping* – I don't find that outlet shopping is that much cheaper than the regular stores, except on holidays. I always find ridiculous bargains during the holidays.

- *Search for Coupons* – Download coupon apps on your phone and Save, Save, Save! Shop the clearance racks for your next season wear – My #1 secret shopping tip is to shop off-season. For example, I purchase almost all of my summer apparel in the winter and vice versa. I save a ton of money!

The next time you show up for work or attend a networking event you can walk in the room in style without breaking the bank.

The Power Of Networking

One of the most critical steps to reaching your potential is building relationships through networking. Before I joined the corporate world, I used to hear the term "networking" and thought of a sea of people at a function, putting their best foot forward, armed with a pocket full of business cards. Of course there was networking in the world of modeling but it was always more casual than I imagined it to be in corporate America. However, I realized that, no matter what industry or background you come from, the most important element of networking is building relationships with people you will potentially be doing business with. People do business with people they know, like and trust. While I think networking should be an organic process, there are two steps I suggest in order to make it more intentional and purposeful:

- ***Never make networking all about you.*** Paul C. Brunson is a Mentor, Entrepreneur and Television Host. Before becoming the powerhouse that he is today, he was an assistant to the ultimate powerhouse: Oprah Winfrey. During a conference speech, he shared an example of one of the many emails he received on a regular basis. It read something like, "Hi Paul, I'm working on an incredible opportunity and project. Could you introduce me to Oprah?" He went on to say that he receives about fifty emails like this a week from people he never met. Despite not knowing him, they feel this is a proper introduction. They basically expect something for nothing. Networking should never be thought of as, what can you do for me? Or what can I do for you situation? I like to believe networking is a mutually beneficial interaction that has the potential to lead to an equitable relationship. Just like any other relationship, you should never go into it with a "What can I get from this person" mentality. I agree with Paul's perspective when it comes to networking his motto, "I give, give, give, give, give, give and *then* I ask." He is constantly looking at providing for the other person. This explains why he is highly successful today.

- ***Maximize opportunities while minimizing your time.***
One day I took it upon myself to approach one of the lawyers I worked with, telling him I wanted to enhance my career in the industry. I said to him, quite frankly, "I want to make a million dollars. What would you suggest?" As you can see, I believe in being very specific and getting straight to the point. His response, "I want you to get into business development and it's going to start with networking. I want to invite you to attend an event with me next week." Instantly I was excited, I didn't expect such an immediate response! I asked how many people would be there? He responded, "500." I nodded my head and thanked him without flinching, but internally I was thinking 500 people! I thought how am I going to network with 500 people? Immediately, I went back to my office and came up with a plan. I knew our firm purchased two tables at the event and I would be seated at one of the tables. I instantly thought to myself, "Maria, get a seating chart." Once I had the chart in hand, I saw that there were going to be nine other potential clients at the table with me, so I researched them beforehand. I was determined to make this networking opportunity a success. During the networking hour, I found two of the nine people who were assigned to sit at my table and connected with them on a surface level. Once we got to the table, I was able to engage them with confidence because I knew who they were before they even introduced themselves. "Oh yes, you're Hillary!" I said to one of the women at the table. "I loved your television show and your recent article!" Hillary, along with everyone else at the table, was very impressed that I had done my homework.

People love talking about themselves. All I did was ask questions, actively listen, and take notes in my head. Having this knowledge ahead of time allowed us to get all of the foundational business talk out of the way (who you are, what you do, etc.) and allowed us to quickly get to the relationship building portion of networking. By the end of the night, I knew the number of children the lady sitting next to me had, the schools they attended, sports they played, things that I couldn't have looked up online. All of this information came as a result of her feeling like she could be free to talk about other dynamics that mattered to her. Although they didn't know who I was at the beginning of the dinner, they wanted to know me by the end. This taught me that there are going to be business meetings, conferences and events I will attend that may be overwhelming in size and that networking with everyone isn't realistic. However, it's very possible to have fifteen-minute intentional conversations with about nine to ten people. Never try to work the entire room. If the opportunity is presented ahead of time, select a few people attending the event, learn about them and nurture those relationships by being prepared, engaged, and attentive.

Ask Great Questions

When I first started in the corporate world, networking wasn't something I looked forward to, but now I find it fun and an amazing opportunity to learn about other people. I understand for some, that initial moment of breaking the ice with someone can be a little intimidating. Although people love to talk about themselves, they do not necessarily want to be the ones to initiate the conversation. Therefore, I find it helpful to always have a couple of questions ready to ask someone about themselves outside of what they do. Once the intros are out of the way, I like to take the opportunity to ask more thought provoking questions. Let me share a few examples of what I mean.

- I met a young woman at an event and in the midst of our conversation, I could tell her mind was somewhere else. It wasn't that she wasn't present, her energy was just off. So I asked her, *"If you could be anywhere else right now, where would you be?"* She replied, "I would rather be home with my daughter. She is sick and I really want to be there with her; however, my business is suffering so I'm trying to make some new connections." As a working mother myself, I could understand. Trying to give 100% at both home and work can be a challenge. I knew exactly how she was feeling. This was an instance where networking isn't always about just knowing what someone does. At that moment, she had a need that outweighed business. She was in need of a support system that could help her. I shared with her about a group of single parent women, some of whom are my clients, who formulated a circle of support for one another's children for when they have to travel on business or attend evening events. I offered to put her in contact with them. Serving others will never cost you anything when you do it from the heart.

- Another question I like to ask at networking functions is one that I often use when I'm interviewing someone: *"What are you passionate about?"* Most of the time people will always reference work. Essentially in networking settings, when we get beyond the introductory stage, you would be amazed at what people reveal.

Beyond surface level conversation you can learn so many things that can be helpful to growing a relationship, as well as a business.

Don't Rely On Business Cards

Networking extends beyond passing out business cards. Networking is more about building relationships. After the networking event previously mentioned with over 500 attendees, immediately following the event, I had lunch meetings, and coffee engagements. As a result of those connections, my firm now sponsors a training program by one of the individuals that I connected with. There is a keyword that I want to address here: "immediately." Remember earlier when I mentioned that my impression of networking in the corporate world consisted of a sea of people and business cards? In this instance, that could not have been further from the truth. At this dinner, when I made these connections, there wasn't a single business card exchanged and every lunch meeting and coffee date that I set up was done on the spot. Don't get me wrong, I'm not saying business cards are a waste of time and card stock. I'm simply saying that when it comes to building relationships and moving forward, it has been my experience that you have more success by nailing down a date and time in that very moment rather than passing on a business card in hopes that the person you're trying to connect with will use it as a tool for follow-up. It's all about taking action "in the moment." Business professionals are often meeting new people all the time. Which can make follow-up conversations extremely difficult because the work hours in a day are already packed. Let's say you meet ten new people and you potentially want to have follow-up meetings with five of them. Do you schedule the meeting then or wait? If you wait, the likelihood that you're going to spend an extra couple of hours in your workday trying to get them on the phone or send emails to schedule meetings are slim. And surely, you could take their business card and pass it on to your admin (if you're at the level of having one) when you get back to the office. Even then, you have to take the time to explain the nature of the meeting or initial contact so the email or call isn't too vague. This requires unnecessary time. Establishing next steps on the spot is beneficial for both parties involved. My point is do not rely on business cards as a means of taking the next step. These cards are great for building contact files, however not bridges.

Don't Be A Wallflower

There have been times when I have walked into a room and spotted what I like to call "wallflowers." These are the people who are not engaging with anyone in conversation. Just imagine walking into a networking event and 95% of the people are actively engaging and talking, and you see someone against the wall, on their phone, with a beverage in their hand and not engaging at all. Just think to yourself, would you want to approach this person in the room? I wouldn't. Eliminate all devices and distractions, or what I like to call, "crutches" and engage. All you have to do is just look over at someone, smile, and simply say, "Hello, my name is _____" to open the pathway to a conversation.

Mentorship

When you are starting out in your career journey, seeking mentorship serves as an asset. As a coach I advise the women in my programs on the importance of having a mentor who is where or has been where they are trying to go. I encourage them to watch the people in their industry as a model. I know this sounds cliché; however, I believe if you watch people in your industry it will help you to avoid some of the pitfalls they experienced. I know you're asking, "Maria how do I find the right person?" I thought you would never ask. Here are a few tips: first, it will require you to dive deep into research. Once you find a few people, you must ensure their integrity and leadership align with your core values. If the person you desire as a mentor is either too busy or out of reach, look for other ways they may share information such as; books, podcasts, live broadcasts, speaking engagements, and/or seminars via video or in person where you can access. A mentorship is a two-way partnership. You must be willing and open to learning. Remember, you get out what you put in.

One of my business inspirations is Lisa Nichols. However, Lisa lives on the opposite side of the country and because of her abundance of knowledge and experience, gaining access to her is not an easy thing to do. One year I heard she was going to be on the east coast. I learned of this information because I had developed a great friendship with someone connected to Lisa. Which takes me back to the importance of building relationships. Because of this established relationship I had the honor of being on the front row as a VIP at Lisa's event. It was incredible! At the end of the conference Lisa ended by saying she was going to let twenty people into her room. Once again because of my relationship with a sister friend, *I was in the room!* I was literally sitting across the table from Lisa Nichols as she shared her knowledge and wisdom on how we all could grow personally and within our businesses. There I was, being coached by one of the top coaches in the world. I gained some of the most valuable information and clarity for my business in a matter of hours.

The Wheel To Your Greatness

As humans, it's one of our natural tendencies, even if it's only for a brief period, to focus on the things we do not do well versus focusing on the things we excel at. Climbing the corporate ladder, with merely a high school diploma and a few college credits while working side-by-side with lawyers who had dual degrees, I struggled with believing in myself. I had to make a choice. I could allow my lack of higher education intimidate me, or I could hone in and focus on the skills I did have and improve them to become the expert I knew I could be. That's exactly what I did. I focused my attention on learning everything there was for me to learn in the key areas of my job in Human Resources. I decided that by the time I finished, no one was going to know more in my career field than me. I read every article, researched every association, and connected with the one's that were beneficial to my career path. Without even realizing it, I had made myself an expert leader in my firm. The attorneys with doctorates and engineering degrees were coming to me. As much as they knew about their own fields, they needed my wisdom, advice and expertise when it came to human resources. My drive to focus and hone in on my job and the things I was good at made me a key asset in my firm. I never could have become that go to person if I had continued to doubt myself due to my lack of credentials. I focused on what I knew and I mastered it!

Finding your strengths and improving upon them can make all the difference in the growth of your career. For some, however, I do realize that it may not be that easy to pinpoint exactly what it is you do well. For example in my field, the title "human resource" describes a human being and the skills and talents they bring to the workforce. Of those skills and talents, I knew it would benefit me to pick one or two and master them. I will be honest, it was difficult for me to choose right away. However, as time progressed, I started paying attention to what other people told me I was great at. This will happen to you often during your career trajectory. Colleagues and potential clients will start pointing out the things they notice about you. For me, I was told repeatedly that I was a good interviewer. They would say things like, "Maria, you're such an exceptional interviewer. Where did you come up with that question?" And of course, I'm thinking, "I don't know, I just came up with it." This was something that came naturally to me. Listening to others and asking the right questions. That natural ability (because we all have some natural ability that stands out) is the one thing we should pay attention to. When others point out something you're good at, make note of that strength it could become your area of focus. When I began to focus on developing the very thing people told me I excelled at, that was when I began noticing positive growth and results in my career. I continued to network and meet people, which in return led to me being asked to speak at a human resources conference about interviewing skills. Excelling in one area can lead to building skills in other areas of your life. Remember, nothing happens overnight. My growth happened over a matter of years. It's not just about identifying your key strengths;

you must have the patience to stay the course and allow things to unfold step-by-step.

While working with women through My Sisters CEO, I have come to realize it's not easy for everyone to identify a specific area they can hone in on and perfect. Therefore, I incorporated a tool called "The Wheel of Life."

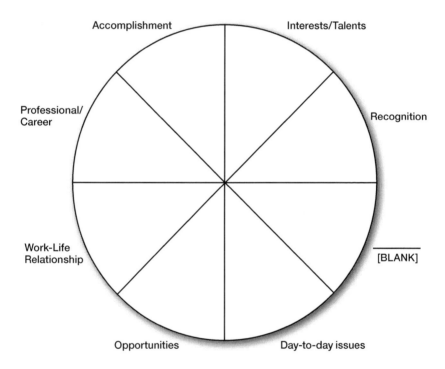

{Seeing the center of the wheel as 0 and the outer edges as 10, rank your level of satisfaction/fulfilment with each area by drawing a line across the wedge. Feel free to place your own heading in the blank wedge. In each area, think about what factors might move your satisfaction up a notch, or several notches?}

The Wheel of Life is designed to walk my clients through an exercise to discover the things that are important to them. This exercise pushes them to visualize starting with the end and working their way back to the beginning. It allows them to be present in the moment. Or, like Stephen Covey said, "I start with the end in mind." So I take my clients through a series of questions allowing them to dig deep within and discover what lies beneath the surface:

- Is your life on track for the success you have imagined for your future self?
- Are you meeting the goals you set for yourself, family, and career?
- What shift do you need to make to re-align your life's mission?
- What are you most proud of up to this point?

This exercise serves as an opportunity for them to have a glance into the future and see the impact they have left on the world. And also build an open and honest relationship with themselves about how they want to show up in the world versus who other people want them to be.

Step 3

3
Challenge Yourself To Do More

We all have that one thing that is a challenge for us to shake; for me it was smoking cigarettes. I hate to admit it, but I enjoyed it. Every day I was reminded of why I needed to quit, however quitting smoking was the hardest thing I ever did! If you would have known me it was contrary to my lifestyle as a fitness junkie. The one thing I enjoyed was keeping me from the very thing I truly loved and that was fitness. Smoking kept me from being able to actively run and jog.

Growing up smoking was a part of my childhood. Everyone smoked! My parents, grandmother, even the clergy. As a little girl, I remember one cold winter night sitting in the backseat of our station wagon with my sisters. The windows were rolled up while both my parents were in the front seat, smoking. I remember taking a deep breath inhaling the vapors of the smoke filled car. I uttered the words, "I love the way that smells." I will never forget the shocked and sad look on my mother's face. My parents' habit of smoking transferred to three of their four daughters. My sister Monica and I both started smoking in high school and we continued on for years. Later in life we both, unannounced to each other decided to stop smoking within weeks of one another. We were both living a smoke-free life for years before Monica was diagnosed with lung cancer, which eventually took her life.

Before she passed away I asked her: "If the Lord healed you and gave you a new lung, what would you do with it?" She replied,

> "I would run." Smiling at the thought she continued: "I would run, and cry, and scream, and keep on running because I don't have the breath to do those things now with only one, barely functioning lung."

In honor of my challenge to do more, I started running in honor of my sister. Granted, it started as just a little jog; however, it felt amazing! Every time I ran I thought of Monica, she was my biggest cheerleader. Six months after her death, I organized a run/walk in memory of my sister. Nearly 100 people joined me for the 5k. I continued to run until eventually the impact of running caused me to injure both of my Achilles. I could barely walk, let alone run any longer. This was devastating to me because I attributed my ability to maintain my weight over the last fifteen years to working out and eating right. I knew I couldn't maintain this by sitting around on my butt. I knew I had to do something different. Society places a lot of pressure on women to maintain their physical health and appearance, especially African American women in high positions. So many of us feel like we have to represent our entire race and gender.

The most uncomfortable place to be is the center of attention when you don't feel confident or comfortable within yourself. My need to make a change in my life led me to join a gym. I noticed a woman trainer working with her client over time and they stood out to me. I could tell that whatever program the trainer had her client on was yielding outer results. I approached her one day and explained my injury and she shared how there are a number of exercises she could work with me on to maintain my weight, as long as I also maintained healthy eating habits.

Needless to say I immediately hired her. Fast forward, a couple of months and I too could see the results. She helped me to strengthen my ankles, legs and feet to the point where I could run again. Rather than immediately returning to running I chose to start power walking. The point of my story is that although I had injured both of my Achilles I didn't count myself out. Instead, I challenged myself to find alternative ways to reach my physical fitness goals. And as a result, I am now stronger than I was before! Here are four key power plays to challenge yourself as you reevaluate, refocus, reset and renew your life.

Re-Evaluate Everything

Hanging on the wall of my office, is a whiteboard where I brainstorm and write my "word for the quarter." By "word," I don't just mean one word. In fact it is a "message." As I gaze over at the board writing today my message is: "Re-evaluate Everything!" This prompted me to share with you that today might be the perfect time to reflect back over everything. Each day, I pause and ask myself, "Did I push the envelope as much as I could? Did I challenge the norm professionally and personally?" I'm a firm believer that just because I have done things a certain way, does not mean I have to continue to do them the same. Sticking to the norm isn't always a proper response. Not only does this type of thinking present a challenge for me, it stands in the way of the managers I supervise, the employees within my company, and my family. That is why I hold myself to a standard of excellence. I constantly re-evaluate by asking myself, "Is there a possibility that I could do things better? Is there room for improvement? Will it push me beyond my comfort zone? Will it allow me to grow personally and professionally?" During my corporate climb and entrepreneurial endeavor I continuously make time to re-evaluate and review my life. When you step back to re-evaluate and re-assess, you often allow for improvement as well as the opportunity to experience a shift in your perspective. I challenge you today to pause and re-evaluate, not just from a career standpoint, but also from a personal level.

Refocus Personally

With the responsibility of working a nine-to-five and running two businesses it's critically important to make time for my husband. He makes sure I don't forget him. Marriage is a lifetime commitment. I had to learn how to find harmony within it all and not have more commitment to my phone. I remember being on family vacation in Florida and I made a vow not to look at my phone. But as soon as my husband stepped out of my sight to quickly run to the car, I was sneaking to check my phone for messages. This irritates my husband to no end. He says things like, "Why are you bringing those people into our bedroom?" Or, "Why are you bringing those people along on our date night?" I had to challenge myself to become more self-aware when it came to not just the phone, but being fully present in every moment. My husband's personal observation truly resonated with me. It was his way of sharing with me that mutual *Respect* was necessary. I realized I was not being an attentive wife when it came to being mindful of respecting him and our time together. I had to challenge myself to manage my workload and not be managed by it. For example, we have date nights typically on Friday's so I tell my assistant I will be unavailable starting at 6:00pm. My assistant understands that I will not check my phone until the next morning. Of course we have a way of communicating in case of an emergency. Having this system in place changed the behavior and expectations of my colleagues, supervisors and clients. Once you respond to calls and requests at night, your actions communicate to the other person that you're available to them *all* the time. I realized in the beginning I created the misalignment in communication and I had to go back and create barriers around my personal time. I call these barriers my personal fences. Fences are intended to protect you and keep the people you want in and the ones you don't want in, out. One of the first fences I put up was to never walk into the house on the phone. This applies to work, business, my girlfriends, family, even my favorite girl, my mother. Believe it or not, EVERYONE understands and respects my fences! I had to become intentional about being present in my marriage.

Working harder doesn't always equal working longer, especially with today's technology. Don't feel that the only way you can prove yourself is to be on call 24/7 for your employer. For entrepreneurs, this can be a little different. Sometimes you find yourself working around the clock, especially if you're just starting out. However, carve out time to reset and take care of yourself as you set boundaries around your private time for family.

Reset Challenges

Even when you think times are difficult always remember there is someone else who is experiencing even tougher times. As the CEO of My Sisters Closet I have had front line encounters of challenges women face. A part of the mission in my organization is to serve women who are in homeless shelters. If you are by any chance wondering what these women look like, take a minute and look in the mirror. They look just like you and I beautiful, brilliant, and brave. The only difference is that many of these women have fallen on hard times. One of the workshops we hosted through My Sisters Closet for the women was

Natural Hair Care Day. We invited a hair stylist to come in and educate the women. They loved it. Not only did they sit and listen to the stylist, but they also asked several questions based upon their experiences with hair care. What I noticed was they were extremely talented when it came to hair styling, care and maintenance. These ladies stepped up and shared some of their hair care tips. Many of them however, had never gone to cosmetology school. So I challenged them to ask how they might be able to obtain grants to attend school as well as what they could do to increase their skills. Unless we are made aware of new possibilities and realities our current situation will keep us stagnant.

I am reminded of a woman who started out in a shelter and today she is working in corporate America and running her own non-profit organization. She didn't allow the lack of financial resources to stop her from catapulting to where she is today. Instead, she dug down deep, discovered what she had and put it to work. I challenge you today, if there is any area in your life that you would love to improve upon, however, you feel something is hindering you, take some time to sit down and examine whether or not you can find ways around it, especially if the obstacle you're facing is financial. There are organizations (mine included) out there ready to support individuals looking to make improvements in their lives through education, resources and funding.

During my time of financial challenges my greatest learning experiences happened. There was a time when I wasn't financially able to invest in furthering my knowledge and training through attending workshops and conferences. I started finding ways to not allow my finances to be an excuse to my growth. I began asking and volunteering – if you never ask, no one will know what you stand in need of. Having the courage to ask allowed me to land a dynamic mentor. Having access to this mentorship helped in all areas of my personal and professional life. I often had to put my pride aside and ask my mentor, what I felt at the time were silly questions. But questions that needed answers. I was willing to be vulnerable and reveal that there were things I didn't know, no matter how big or small. Never be afraid to speak up about what you don't know because many times, the most unsuspecting people have been where you are and are looking for the opportunity to pay it forward, the way someone once helped them. I remember attending a seven-course dinner where a young woman had never had this experience before. I helped her not because I wanted to show off or make her feel less. I just remembered had I not learned I too would not have known which table manners to use during dinner. Being able to help her was a blessing to me just as much as it was to her. Always feel open to ask questions as you journey through life for the purpose of challenging yourself to stretch beyond your comfort zone.

Renew Your Life

As a woman I believe it is important to be a living testament of what you teach and preach to the people you serve. I stress to my clients the importance of staying relevant. Five years ago, I attended my final week of my coaches' certification training; we were placed in pairs for an in-depth personal training exercise. My assigned partner was "in my face" with love and did not allow me to shrink back or play small. She called me out of my victimization mindset of not believing in myself. I will never forget that moment. The training exercise was centered on the mission, vision and goals for serving women through my non-profit. She loved what she was hearing from me and like any good coach, she challenged me in ways that made me very uncomfortable, offering suggestions that frightened me quite frankly because of the level of transparency required on my part. What she was asking would require me to show up big and bold. I didn't have the educational background I thought was needed for the things she was suggesting. Truth be told, her ideas were just bigger than what I planned for myself. Right then, she stopped me dead in my tracks and said,

> "Wait a minute, you can't go out coaching others to be more, do more and be all they can be and you're not doing the very thing you preach. You're a counterfeit and your coaching model is not a truth you are living out. It's just a lie." She stood up from her seat, looking down on me and said, "You can't show up genuinely and authentically to these women if you are believing the lie that you are not good enough. I see you in this room and you are a dynamic speaker."

Then, she did something that really shook me. She got eye-level with me and said,

> "If you can't be totally authentic you need to close that non-profit down right now. You're not genuine, you're not authentic and you have no right to try and inspire these women if you don't believe it yourself."

Of course my first instinct was to be defensive. But she was right. I was encouraging these women to push boundaries and do things bigger than their personal visions and yet, I wasn't ready to do that for myself. The revelation in our talk pushed me at that moment to start writing and speaking affirmations over my life. It was time out for living in fear and believing I wasn't good enough and didn't have what it takes. This was an incredible personal breakthrough moment that catapulted me to another level. It allowed me to stop believing the lies I had been telling myself. I finally accepted that every scripture written about being more than a conqueror, being fearfully and wonderfully made, included me! What if we really renewed our minds to believe that everything the Word of God says about us is true, that God could use us, mess and all? And that every area we are lacking or falling short in is exactly where God wants us so that He can fill every void. *We can do all things through Christ who strengthens us.*

A speaker once said, "The one thing you have been running from all these years, the thing you thought was your kryptonite, that thing you thought was going to kill you, is really your breakthrough." For me, my kryptonite was the fact that I didn't have a college education. If I can be transparent, I was scared to say it out loud. I thought people would believe I was a fraud. Here I am, sitting in boardrooms at the head of the table, with people who have PhDs, JDs, LLMs. The day I realized I deserved a seat in the room was my breakthrough. All along I was self-sabotaging myself and I didn't even realize it. Often the biggest challenge we have to face is that internal struggle of not believing we deserve what God has already assigned to us. We even go as far as to convince ourselves that *everyone* is thinking the same negative thoughts about us that we are. When in fact they have their own internal struggle and they are not thinking about yours. I encourage you to renew your mind, body and spirit by speaking life daily to yourself through affirmations. Those moments when you begin to feel discouraged take out your affirmations and remind your self-sabotaging voice *who's the boss*!

Step 4

4
Commit To You

When you are committed, God is a promise keeper! In the Webster's Dictionary the definition of commitment is "a promise to do or give something." Very early on in life I made the commitment to always give my all. I did everything from reading about the HR Profession to finding a mentor in my field. My commitment spanned for thirty years with my firm, which is something that people in my generation would consider a sign of loyalty. The next generation (Millennials) to dominate the workforce would view my career trajectory from a completely different perspective. They see my experience as limited because I have only been in one place and haven't really experienced anything else. Millennials have been scrutinized for moving from opportunity to opportunity for money thus lacking a sense of commitment. With times changing so rapidly I started to question myself as to whether sticking with one company for thirty years was a smart move. I begin to question if my dedication would be seen as a sign of stagnation rather than a sign of growth. After consideration, I realized my loyalty to the company served not only them but my needs and goals.

Over the years my firm has evolved in offering different opportunities for me due to mergers and acquisitions. During my career in HR, I have worked in all aspects of the field. Each opportunity provided me insight and clarity to taking the position I dreamed of from day one when I walked in and saw the Director of HR at the helm of a major law firm. During my tenure here are four power plays that helped me catapult to the position I desired.

The Grass Isn't Always Greener

In my role, I have experienced what I like to call *boomerangs*. These are colleagues that leave the firm but end up coming back. The best and the brightest are welcomed back with open arms. In fact, they are the best advertisement that we are a great place to work. Some former employees leave thinking the grass is greener on the other side. Often times it can look that way. We have many long tenured employees throughout our firm because as leaders we are committed to the success of our team. I have heard so many stories from the *boomerangs* of the bait and switch trick, where you accept a position that is described as a higher-level role and it turns out to be a completely different job. I found that rehiring boomerangs also boosts morale because they come back sharing the horror stories with other employees, about their experiences. In no way through this example am I saying you shouldn't look for other opportunities when the time comes. However, if you decide to seek other opportunities, I recommend these five steps:

- ***Step 1: Plan Your Exit Strategy*** – If you are considering leaving your current employer to make more money, plan financially for an extended lapse before receiving your first paycheck. Giving two weeks advance notice to your employer is customary and common courtesy.

- ***Step 2: Anticipate A Counter Offer*** – Consider the possibility of your company making a counter offer for more money or a new position. Would you consider staying? What are the non-negotiable areas that must be included in the counteroffer?

- ***Step 3: Compare Benefits*** – One of the top mistakes boomerangs said they failed to do was consider the benefits and out-of-pocket costs. With rising health care expenses more companies are pushing the increases to the employees through higher premium costs, exorbitant deductibles and more. Other costs, like parking, train/bus fares should be considered.

- ***Step 4: Set Long-Term Goals*** – In preparing for your next opportunity ensure that it offers the trajectory to climb the ladder with in your career goals. Moving to a new job for more money into a role that is not aligned to your strengths, passion and career goals can be paralyzing.

- ***Step 5: Get Clear About What You Want*** – Seeking clarity about what is most important to you may sound simple but most job seekers do not take the time to consider this in advance and regret doing so.

In the end, the decision is ultimately your choice. My goal is to ensure you have the tools to successfully make an informed decision. In making life decisions your first point of commitment should be to your personal success.

Make the Decision to Commit

As you explore career paths it can be tricky to hone in on what to commit your time and energy to. As a receptionist at the front desk I had a clear view of everything going on in the office. As I watched the HR director, I said to myself, "I want that job." Having the opportunity to serve her assistants gave me an inside view of what it would be like as I envisioned myself doing the job. In the Bible, Habakkuk 2:2, God instructs Habakkuk, "Write down the vision and make it plain." And that's what I did. I wrote down the vision of what was required of me to obtain my dream job. Once I discovered my sweet spot for interviewing my confidence grew stronger. I realized I was on the right track in my career serving in areas I am naturally good at. My career didn't "fall into place" overnight it took me seven years. During that time I wasn't doing groundbreaking work. In fact I spent most of the time performing what most would consider menial, administrative tasks before finding my sweet spot. The great part about the journey was that I served in the department I desired to grow in. I had a bird's eye view. I was first in line to volunteer to take over the tasks that most didn't like doing. I can recall a period when one of our senior supervisors had the distressing task of filling last minute overtime requests. At the end of the day she would begin by going down a list, calling every secretary in the office to find someone who was willing to stay late to support a deal closing, litigation support, or some other intense project. After about a week of watching this play out, I raised my hand to volunteer to make the calls for her. As you can imagine she was thrilled to off-load the responsibility to me. Eventually it became a function of my job and not only did I take it over, I found a way to make it more efficient. Normally the coordinator would call around about twenty minutes before closing to find someone, but I checked in with the secretaries early in the day, providing an opportunity for them to make arrangements for extended childcare or other home responsibilities. Throughout my career I positioned myself so that the people who could make the decisions would notice my level of commitment to the company. Being fully committed is necessary in order to yield greater results. People say, "It's not about what you know, it's about who you know." I disagree, I believe, "It's not about who you know but who knows you."

Commit To Your Personal Growth

I believe in working just as hard at being a successful wife and mother as I do at building a career. It has *not* always been easy. My husband and I went through some very difficult times at a point in our marriage. We weren't perfect by any means. However, thirty-three years later, we are committed. I remember having an argument and our emotions were running high; I told him I wanted him to leave. He reverted back to our vows and he said,

> "I would never leave you. If you want to go, just know I don't want you to go, but I'm not leaving."

Thank God for that being his response, I wouldn't have let him leave anyway. We were committed to one another despite the hard times. When most people might have said, "To hell with it, I'm done." He didn't walk away and neither did I. My husband was not only committed to our marriage, he was committed to our children and the Stanfield name. I struggled for many years, comparing our marriage to others that appeared happier and sunk into a state of self-pity. It wasn't until I applied the Word of God to my marriage that things started to change for the better. I took the focus off of Kevin and me and turned my attention on ways to better myself within our marriage. A Biblical principle states, "Honor and submit to our husbands, not only when and if they do everything right, but always so that we can be a reflection of God's love." When I started pouring into self-care things started to turn around in my life. The changes I made overflowed into my children. I saw them modeling some of my behaviors. That was a blessing. Children model everything we show them. They are more likely to do what we do rather than do what we say. For so long I was hard on myself, but God had plans of honoring my family and life in ways I could have never imagined.

I have been blessed to witness people through My Sister CEO, step into higher levels of commitment in their lives. Many times when working with clients I find they often are just doing things for the sake of doing. When in reality their true passion is hidden beneath, waiting to be awakened. Frustrated and stagnate, I had a client who was anxious and determined to shift but didn't know how. I walked her through one of my signature coaching visualization exercises causing her to move from where she was to the very thing that keeps her heart beating. I reminded her that in life you will either land or fall, but the most important part is that you have the courage to take the step. Mid-way through the exercise she had an ah-ha moment. She committed to pursuing her dreams and now doors are opening beyond her imagination.

Are you at a point in your life where you are feeling stuck? If so, let's climb to the top of your cliff and discover your next level by answering the following question:

What are some ways in which you have demonstrated your commitment to success?

Personally

_____

_____

_____

_____

_____

_____

_____

Business

_____

_____

_____

_____

_____

_____

_____

Career

_____

_____

_____

_____

_____

_____

Your dreams are waiting for you to show up, grab hold of your courage and take the first step.

Don't Dim Your Light

Just like faith, sometimes commitment can make you come across as arrogant, or audacious. Not everyone is committed to what it takes, to show that they believe in themselves. For myself, my commitment first and foremost is to God. He requires that we do all things with excellence because our job here on earth is to be His representatives. That's first in my mind anytime I set out to do something. I am not worried about how other people view my level of commitment. Now, I have not always been that confident but as my relationship has grown with God, it has empowered me to step out in faith. Matthew 5:16 states: "Let your light so shine before men, that they may see your good works, and glorify your Father which is in heaven." Always remember your confidence is not dependent upon someone else's view of you. If they can't handle your shine it doesn't mean you should dim your light!

Step 5

5
Elevate Your Mindset

Recently through my company, My Sister CEO, I worked with a mother who struggled for years to get her daughter to elevate her mindset. Following up with a post I made on social media about a job opportunity the mother reached out hoping I could help her daughter polish her interview skills. At the age of twenty-nine she had experienced a difficult life journey many of us could never imagine. I sat down with her and asked her to share her story and as she began speaking the tears streamed down her face. She began to share that in her senior year of high school she became pregnant and was unable to attend college. Her not attending college after high school was an immediate connection and a commonality we shared. After graduating she had no other choice but to find a job to care for herself and the baby. Unfortunately, her mother at the time put her out the house. It was a difficult decision to make. It was one of those situations where we hear all too often that sometimes we have to let our children learn on their own. She did everything from bartending, braiding hair, waiting tables and eventually, dancing for money. Things got tough at times causing her to live in hotels and shelters. In that moment, hearing her story I could hear and see that she was a survivor. As she continued to cry I didn't rush to console her. Instead I asked her what's making you cry? She responded,

> "I have done things in my life that I am too ashamed to even disclose."

I reminded her of the natural instinct of every mother to do whatever it takes to care for her child. I looked her straight in the eyes and told her, "No one is going to hire you if you can't tell your story without crying. Your past is your past and you cannot change it. The reason you are here is because you have decided to shift and change your future and it's time to stop wallowing in your story and stand on your story." I brought to mind for her the visual of Wonder Woman and how she stands triumphantly with hands on her hips, chest out, and chin up, ready to conquer the world. I made her stand up, face-to-face with me and told her to repeat: *I am standing on top of my story.* I told her to create sticky notes with the words, "strong" and "resilient", along with a few others. I told her to put the sticky notes all around her. I said to her, "now, *I'm* going to tell you your story." I shared her story from a place of power, strength and resilience. I shaped her story from a victor's viewpoint and not a victim. I had her stand in the mirror and repeat her story five times. She felt empowered.

As a gift, I purchased her an interview outfit she could wear. I know all to well what it's like to wear second hand clothes. Now that I am in a place where God has blessed me so that I can be a blessing to others. It is so much more than buying an outfit it is about supporting another woman in her journey. When she tried on that dress she felt like a confident woman ready to embark upon a new (and for her, probably scary) direction in her life for herself and daughter.

When it was time for her interview, she was surprised that I was sitting in the room when she walked in. When she sat down, I didn't say anything. I just sat back and allowed my manager to handle all the interview questions. When she opened her mouth to tell her story, I was in awe! She told her story with such courage. I was extremely proud of her but I couldn't show it in the interview. I wanted to jump up, hug her and give her a high five but that's definitely not professional. I'm glad to say that a couple of days after she interviewed, she was offered the job.

What I gathered from her story was that she was always a force to be reckoned with. Look at everything she went through in order to provide for her child. She's a survivor and that is a trait of someone with a growth mindset. Survivors think on their feet and are always ready to adapt to change. Instead of continuing to make lateral life moves just to stay steady, she made a vertical one to take her higher. In her case, it was something as simple as making the decision not to allow her lack of education to continue keeping her stagnant. I can relate to this young woman's story, because until a few years ago, I felt like I *needed* a college education in order to prove myself to the world. I thank God He doesn't settle for His children determining their worth according to the world's standards.

One day during my devotion time God spoke to me through His word in the Book of John 5:1-9 where it tells the story of the man at the pool of Bethesda:

> Verse 1: Later on there was a feast of the Jews, and Jesus went up to Jerusalem.

Verse 2: Now there is in Jerusalem near the Sheep Gate a pool with five covered colonnades, which in Aramaic is called Bethesda.

Verse 3: On these walkways lay a great number of the sick, the blind, the lame, and the paralyzed.

Verse 4: From time to time an angel of the Lord would come down and stir up the waters. The first one into the pool after each such disturbance would be cured of whatever disease they had.

Verse 5: One man there had been an invalid for thirty-eight years.

Verse 6: Jesus saw him lying there and realized he had already been there a long time. "Do you want to get well?" He asked.

Verse 7: "Sir," replied the sick man, "I have no one to help me into the pool when the water is stirred. While I am on my way, someone else goes in before me."

Verse 8: Then Jesus told him, "Get up, pick up your mat, and walk."

Verse 9: Immediately the man was made well, and he picked up his mat and began to walk.

Through this story God revealed to me how He has already given me permission to take up my own mat and walk. He told me I don't need a college education. So while I was wallowing in lack, God was (and still is) showing me in every area of my life that a piece of paper doesn't determine who I am. I have grown; however, I must admit sometimes I do circle back to that pool of Bethesda, questioning myself. Today, I realize every area in my life where I felt I was lacking, God wanted me to lean on Him even more.

Are you in a space where you are feeling defeated if so here are a few reflection questions for you to answer.

Do you need a mindset shift?

_____

_____

_____

_____

_____

_____

What do you feel is holding you back?

_____

_____

_____

_____

_____

_____

How can you navigate beyond that?

_____

_____

_____

_____

_____

_____

Below are three power tips to help elevate your mindset…

The Power Of Your Thoughts

Proverbs 23:7: "For as a man (or woman) thinks in his heart, so is he/she. Basically, this means your actions and behavior are a result of your thoughts." Have you ever noticed when you are focused on eating healthy you begin to think about French Fries, Pizza, and/or that big fat Burger? In instances like this we have to check our stinky thinking. Is what's on your mind in alignment with your goal? If not, redirect your thoughts to positivity. Focus on where you want to go and the rest will follow.

The Power Of Your Words

Proverbs 18:21: "Death and Life are in the power of the tongue and those who love it will eat its fruit." I don't know about you but I want to eat the fruit of life. So I speak positive words that give life. Several years ago I started really paying attention to what I was saying and realized how negative I sounded. I was speaking phrases that were contrary to my personality, faith and beliefs such as, "you almost gave me a heart attack," "I can't stand," "I'm sick and tired of." The words we speak reverberate in our hearts and minds, so it's important to engage in positive self-talk. Change your words Change your life!

The Power Of Believing

Matthew 21:22: *"And whatever things you ask in prayer, believing you will receive."* This scripture was hard for me to wrap my head around. You could say I had a hard time believing. I started journaling about all the things God promises me in His word. We must have faith in ourselves we are stronger and more amazing than we think we are. We must become our greatest cheerleader and stop selling ourselves short. We are amazing!

Now that you have had an opportunity to reflect and take back the power of your thoughts, words and beliefs it is time to take action.

Confidently write down a dream that is bigger than anything you have ever done before and remember that no goal or dream is out of reach.

_____

_____

_____

_____

_____

_____

Step 6

6
Stand In Your Confidence

Confidence: A feeling of self-assurance arising from one's appreciation of one's own abilities or qualities

People often judge one's confidence around how much they have accomplished, what they are lacking, and what they have or have not done. Tony Schwartz, President and CEO of The Energy Project and the author of the book *Be Excellent At Anything*, had this to say about being confident: "Very few people succeed in business without a degree of confidence. Yet everyone, from young people in their first real jobs to seasoned leaders in the upper ranks of organizations have moments, days, months, or even years, when they are unsure of their ability to tackle challenges." I can absolutely say I know this to be true from my personal experiences.

Growing up I struggled with my self-confidence. My peers made sure of that. When I was eleven-years-old I remember my parents working two jobs, nights and weekends in order to save the money to purchase their first home. To say that my three sisters and me were excited is putting it mildly. Living in a two-bedroom apartment, with all four girls in one room we were *beyond* thrilled that we were finally moving into a larger home with more bedrooms. As the two oldest, Monica, (the first born) and I shared a room, while the two youngest, Marcie (second from the youngest) and Martina (the baby girl) shared a room. Sharing rooms were fertile ground for blossoming even deeper sisterly bonds.

We all settled into our new neighborhood and made friends quite easily. I met my best friend Lavern. We spent most summer afternoons hanging out talking and giggling for hours about our favorite topic *boys*. We spent our afternoons sitting on the front porch at either her house or mine. Everything on that day was going so well. Whispers and uncontainable laughter permeated the atmosphere as Lavern and I sat on her front porch sharing our secret crushes and the goofy attempts we made that week to get their attention. I never imagined that in an instant everything could change. One moment, one sound, one glimpse, changed my life forever and in many respects, rattled my confidence. Suddenly we heard a loud BANG! It startled us both. We looked back and it was the screen door of my house. My mother stumble backwards out the door, wearing only a white slip that was drenched in blood from her bloody nose. She was screaming for my sisters and I to come home. I leaped up in a hurry from Laverne's front porch and frantically ran toward my mother. My father jumped in his car passing me with his eyes glazed over and drove off. That was the last day my father lived with us.

We no longer had both of our parents living in one home.

Despite my father being away he remained a big part of our lives. His absence in the home caused a huge shift in our family dynamic and my confidence. I went from an extremely confident teen to questioning everything about myself. Years later, as I prepared for my senior year I remember my classmates talking about college. With my poor grades and the financial burden of living in a single parent household with four girls, college wasn't a serious discussion or possibility for me. With my father out of the home my only choice was to enter the workforce. I worked as a restaurant hostess, waitress and even a cook flipping burgers. I even tried my hand at a pottery store, doing whatever I could to earn money and not be a financial burden to my mother.

After years of working odd jobs I landed a position in the corporate arena as a receptionist. With only a high school education, my confidence level was stuck within a fifteen-year-old's mindset while living in a woman's body. I was confident in my ability to do the job. However, what concerned me was the uncertainty of: was I good enough and would I be respected? Working for high profile lawyers earning millions with credentials I never heard of intimidated me to say the least. Despite holding my own and landing promotions that insecurity demon frequently reared its ugly head. I remember during company meetings I would sit in the back trying to go unnoticed. Which was hard to do since I am a tall African American woman. Not to mention I was often the only one present in the room. I would sit back, observe and hardly ever speak up. I would just agree with what everyone said, even the conflicting opinions in the room. I quickly realized my lack of confidence of "fitting in" was keeping me from putting my best foot forward. I knew I had to fix this quickly because I was *not* going to lose out on a great opportunity.

Walk In Faith

One of the most famous idioms people love to throw out, "Fake it till you make it" this sounds great but I prefer not to live by it. The idiom means that by faking whatever it is we feel we are lacking, such as confidence, optimism, self-esteem, etc, we will actually manifest these qualities into our lives. My approach is "*faith it* until you make it." I am a woman of faith. I know that my confidence lies within the woman God created me to be and the gifts He bestowed upon me. When I offer the world my gifts, I am not only representing Maria, but I am also representing Christ. The Bible tells us that we are fearfully and wonderfully made. It can often be difficult to take hold of these promises when the world is constantly reminding us who they believe we are or we should be.

We often believe that what others say about us matter, however the words you speak to yourself carry more weight. The word of God says there is power in your tongue. We read the promises in God's word, yet putting them into action well, that's another story. The question remains, how do you begin the process of positive reinforcement to boost your confidence so that it shows up through you on a daily basis? The answer is simple: Daily Affirmations.

Sharing daily affirmations have become an impactful part of my life. I promise they work. Affirmations are not just about writing down positive quotes that sound good on a piece of paper and reciting them. Instead they should have purpose. Here are two important areas to identify in preparing your affirmations: know your foundation and identify your gifts and talents.

- **Know Your Foundation** What does it mean to know your foundation? I believe it is knowing what the guiding principles are for your life and what you stand for. My foundation in my life is Christ. However, my foundation came with challenges as I worked to discover who I was. It wasn't until I became quiet in my life and started listening to God's voice that I began to receive the entire blessings He had in store for me. I can remember a point in my life at the onset of my career when I felt like the weight of the world was on my shoulders. For years during the recession while my husband was unemployed, I was the sole financial provider in my household. That was one of the hardest times in my life. I felt like I was juggling multiple balls at once. Things just weren't working out the way I expected them to. I felt helpless. One day, I just couldn't take it anymore, I went before God, totally transparent and cried out to him, "God, what am I supposed to do?" The Lord said, "I already told you what to do. I told you to start My Sisters Closet." What! Really God? With all the financial pressure I was under I couldn't image where the funds to start a non-profit were going to come from. When you believe things are at its lowest God has a way of revealing your highest moment, even when you don't understand how. God revealed to me that it was time to start a non-profit, a vision He had given me ten years prior. I had no idea how this could be the answer to my current situation. However, I knew I had to be obedient to His message. I knew that every time I followed God's voice, everything always worked out. I stepped out on faith and said, "yes" to God and everything started to fall into place. Doors started to open that I would have never been able to open on my own. One month before the launch of my business, my company offered me the opportunity to attend a career-coaching program. The program cost thousands of dollars. There was no way I could afford to participate on my own, but this is how God shows up in your life when you trust and respond to Him with obedience. This was another door God opened. The training turned out to be a three-fold blessing for me: it was gifted by my firm, it increased my knowledge and skillset on the job, and it gave me insight into career coaching and training that I in return could use with my clients at My Sisters Closet. In life we have to find our source and draw from our guiding principles.

- **Identify Your Gifts/Talents** When you align with your foundation that is when you will discover your gifts and talents. We often miss out because we become so familiar with the things we know how to do, that we often overlook our unique gifts. What I discovered is that no one can ever be you, no matter how hard they try. You are uniquely you. Start focusing on what you do well, rather than what the world thinks you should be doing. Begin to declare your greatness. It is waiting on you.

Affirmations

Take time today and write down what you stand in need of at this phase of your life. Once you have identified what they are begin to write down action steps needed for them to come to past. Now, take it a step further and write out positive statements declaring it is already done. Hang them in areas that you can see in front of you everyday. Begin to speak them into existence. Remember we believe what we say about ourselves *before* we believe what anyone else says. I have sticky notes, on my bathroom mirror, computer, on my walls, desk, everywhere! Some of my sticky notes say, *"Stop getting ready, be ready, Look for opportunity, Promise to live and to give, I am the sum total of my choices I make today, and I am the CEO of my life."* My affirmations, quotes and scriptures are a daily reminder that I am deserving of all God has in store for me.

Embrace The New You

When you discover and embrace the new you it can be a struggle. As women we fear people will view us as being *arrogant*. I believe confidence and arrogance are totally different. When you have done the work you have a right to shine your high beams. For a long time, in fact until I was working on this book I often struggled with shining my high beams brightly because I didn't want others to believe I was bringing focus to me. One day my dear friend Nicole said,

"Wow, Maria, you look so amazing in that suit!"
I said, "Girl, this suit cost me $5 at a yard sale." Right away my friend reprimanded me and said,

"Stop doing that," she told me. "No one has to know. Just receive the compliment."

It was a powerful statement. I didn't fully receive it at the time, however today I embrace the message and share it with my clients. I learned that if I don't celebrate me, who else will? For so long I would deflect when people would give me a compliment. Instead I realized I should graciously and confidently own my God given greatness.

Now You Know

Once I learned to listen and trust the voice of God, I discovered my purpose. My confidence started to shine through in my business and my job. When I made the decision to name my business My Sisters Closet, so many people tried to convince me that I should choose a different name. I didn't allow them to alter what God had spoken to me and that was to name my non-profit, My Sisters Closet. I decided to focus on the only important voice and that was the voice of God.

Even in my job I listened to God's voice as He whispered, "Maria it is time to come out of hiding in the corner. It is time for you to own the power of your position." My boss played a huge role in helping me to build my confidence as I silently watch him lead. My presence in the board room today is different from the woman who lacked confidence. Today I sit up straight, with my shoulders back and relaxed as I sit at the head of the table.

When you begin to embrace your confidence from within it will shine bright on the outside. It will show up in ways you can't even imagine. People will recognize that there is something different about you and want to know the secrets of what you did to get to that space in your life. In order to get there, it is important for you to tap into your inner-most thoughts, elevate your mindset and watch things begin to unfold in your life.

Step 7

7
Stay Relevant

In 2000 Reed Hastings, the founder of a fledgling company called Netflix, flew to Dallas to propose a partnership to Blockbuster CEO, John Antioco and his team. The idea was that Netflix would run Blockbuster's brand online and Antioco's firm would promote Netflix in its stores. Hastings was laughed out of the room. We all know what happened next. Blockbuster went bankrupt in 2010 and Netflix is now a $28 billion dollar company. About ten times what Blockbuster was worth. Today, Haskins is widely known as a genius and Antioco is considered a fool. We are in a perpetual cycle of change that has become the new norm. From self-checkout lines replacing grocery store cashiers, to online banking replacing bank tellers. If you don't stay relevant, you lose. You can look at our current society and see firsthand how the companies that have adapted to new waves of technology in order to provide better customer service are winning. Blockbuster made a mistake that cost them billions. Where did Blockbuster go wrong, you wonder? They became complacent. They saw what was working for them and they didn't want to budge from it. Maybe they weren't paying attention to the impatient customers waiting in long lines just to check out a video. They frowned upon the red boxes outside the 7-Eleven. They laughed at the idea of having a more convenient, quicker way for customers to access home movie entertainment. They didn't have the foresight to see what was on the horizon.

For corporations and small businesses alike, it is important to stay abreast of the changing market place and how your company, as well as yourself, can adapt with the changes. I could share hundreds of stories with you about workplace relevancy; such as the time I was asked if I was interested in taking over the social responsibility and diversity program for my law firm. I would have had the opportunity to learn new skills, travel the world and lots of other glitzy offerings, but I turned it down. Not because I didn't think it was important or could enhance my skills and workforce relevance, it just didn't align with my career goals and professional future. As a result of my decision to decline the internal offer, the firm decided to hire a candidate from outside the firm and I was assigned as her mentor. Almost immediately after the hire and implementation of this new position the firm won numerous awards and accolades such as Best Places to Work, Top Law Firm in Pro Bono and tremendous notoriety for Diversity and Inclusion. These were quite impressive results; however, a few years later after the hire, the position was eliminated. Great results but not relevant to business operation during a downturn in the economy. Now for me, during this period I was in the background supporting, learning and creating new programs for my local office, while working in my full time leadership position. I stayed relevant. In fact it was during this time that my efforts were noticed and I won the Working Mother of the Year Award. Now I didn't have a crystal ball to forecast the future to know the position would be eliminated, but I learned not to be distracted by what one might call bright shining objects. Here are four important factors I learned from this experience:

- **Trust your instincts** – At the time of the initial offer, I had been with the company long enough to understand success drivers, essential operations, and economy trends. Using my best judgment I made an informed decision to decline the offer. I didn't have a vision board or a goals list like I do today, but I knew beyond a shadow of a doubt that this position was good, but not good for me. I wanted the top role, Director of Administration and this job was not on the roadmap to my career goal. It all came down to me trusting my gut and believing in the collection of my knowledge, subconscious and experiences, as well as my faith in God's guidance. Those 4:00 a.m. talks with God weren't for nothing!

- **Be a life-long learner** – I work for a prestigious and highly successful law firm that hires only the best and brightest lawyers and staff, and because of that, I maintain a student mindset. At work we are encouraged to be perpetual students making contributions and supporting the growth of others. Although I was assigned as the mentor, I was also the mentee, asking questions and watching. There were dozens of new programs, ideas and teachable moments that I gleaned from this partnership that helped accelerate me personally and professionally. Don't be afraid to ask questions, seek advice, and share. Be a team player, it will serve you well.

- **Don't shrink back** – Get noticed. I was asked if I was interested in this position because I created a personal and business brand of professionalism that got me noticed. If you are not visible in pertinent circles, you run the risk of getting overlooked for opportunities that would be highly beneficial to your career trajectory. Note: It was the mentee that recommended my name be submitted for the Working Mother of the Year Award and I won!

- **Be flexible** – Try new ideas and experiment with creative solutions. Fear of failing is a rope of bondage for many who fall behind in the workforce. When thinking of new (sometimes crazy) ideas that no one else could visualize as successful, I am reminded of a story I read about Mr. Walt Disney and his idea about a mouse (Mickey Mouse) and an amusement park. Walt Disney died before Disney World was completed, but at the opening of the park an admirer leaned over to Mrs. Disney and said, "it's such a shame that Walt didn't live to see his dream come true." Mrs. Disney replied, Oh! Walt Disney "saw" his vision before anyone else did. He was a high school dropout who was fired from his first job because they said he lacked creativity and imagination. Walt Disney failed many times but he was always moving forward trying new things. Think of how you can remain flexible by pushing the envelope and testing new ideas. Stay open-minded to creative thinkers. I work with a young woman who's nearly half my age. Her enthusiasm, creativity and technology savvy is a breath of fresh air and keeps me relevant and keenly aware of generational differences and needs in the workplace. We can brainstorm new initiatives from different angles that allow us to consider a great population of our internal and external clients. Hiring her was one of the best decisions I made.

When taking the time to map out your goals to reach your future self, it is important to remain true to your spiritual, professional, and personal values. While it is beneficial to be flexible in your career profession, that doesn't mean you have to compromise. In a society where it seems like anything goes, doesn't mean you have to go with it.

Staying Relevant In Social Media

Social media plays a huge part in the relevancy of a company and/or individual brand today. There are so many tools that can be used to our advantage as business owners. However, if we are not careful, we can end up dedicating too much time to resources that may not be helpful or specific to our business model. I was given an invaluable piece of advice by one of my coaches early on in my business and it was to make sure I knew who my target audience was. Snapchat is a very popular form of social media; however, my target market is not on that platform. It's important to research and identify where your target audience hangs out. This is also part of an exercise I do with my clients for business development and brand identity. I help them discover who their target audience is and where they would spend most of their time on the Internet in order to put together an effective social media marketing strategy. You could have the best marketing strategy, however, if you are on the wrong platform it's not going to help you. And please understand that when we talk about "staying relevant" on social media, it doesn't mean just jumping on there and interacting with people about anything. There must be a certain amount of interaction with your target audience, but I like to call it "interacting with intention." Get involved with conversations and topics relevant to your brand. Join threads and conversations of the people you know who would be interested in your product or services while keeping you in mind when your ideal client is looking for what you offer.

Staying Relevant In Your Personal Life

When I first started out in my career working from home was not an option like it is today. You had to show up to work and put in long hours and work weekends. I remember one day tears began to fill up my eyes as I reflected upon the times I was unable to be present at my girls' games and late to arrive to special events all because I was working. It's hard to admit that I let work get in the way of being fully present with my family because I was trying to prove that I was capable, smart enough, and educated enough to excel at climbing the corporate ladder. My daughters tell me all the time how proud they are of me and I'm so pleased to hear those words from them because they sacrificed mommy time for me to get here.

The most important thing you can focus on in order to keep yourself relevant among your family is to be fully present. There is no pause button in life so we can't go back and catch up. We have to be intentional to keep the people and things in proper alignment. My day begins at 4:00 a.m. with prayer and bible study. By 5:00 a.m. I'm out the door for my morning workout. The double blessing was the day I noticed my daughters modeling my morning prayer and bible study time. My heart still leaps with joy at the thought of it. After my morning run, I check emails and spend quality time with my husband as we prepare to get out the door. I have an elder parent, who has been my best friend since birth, my mother, Mary. She's a handful and I love her. She stays on the go but she lives alone and it is comforting to me to hear her voice and to know that she is safe. Since the passing of my beautiful oldest sister/friend/confidant, Monica, my mom and I talk religiously everyday. We have our time during my commute from work. It takes me about an hour and I make that "me and mommy" time. My mom knows when she hear our crazy dog barking with happiness in the background, it's time to hang up the phone. Whether you are married or single, you need to put boundaries in place for others to respect your time.

My daughters, are now at the age where the most important thing they require from me is my love, attention and an ear to listen. Simply being around them inspires me. We love spending time together as a family, so much so we decided to no longer buy gifts at Christmas and instead create new memories through travel experiences. This is our way of staying relevant as we create our family legacy. This will be the first year our one-year-old granddaughter, Blaire will partake in the experience. We are all super excited! In the end, your family and friends don't really care about how you saved the day at work, or the designer items you purchased as gifts. They care about your presence. Remember to always be present for what matters most in your life.

The Best Is Yet To Come

In this book, I have been completely transparent allowing you into the secret places of my insecurities, challenges, triumphs and breakthroughs as a testament that no matter what adversity you face or your educational background, You Got This! During my journey *From The Front Desk To The Corner Office* I never allowed myself to get caught up in what the world wanted for me, instead I stayed focused on what was important to me.

We are amazing people, described by God as fearfully and wonderfully made. Start believing that for yourself. Today, take the limits off. Dream BIG and walk into your Best Life!

Maria Stanfield
Senior Executive, CEO, Career Coach, Speaker

A native Washingtonian, Ms. Maria Stanfield is a Senior Executive in Corporate America, CEO, Career Coach, Speaker, and founder of My Sisters Closet and My Sister CEO. Maria is passionate about carrying the torch of the women whose shoulders she stand on, which is what led her to birthing My Sisters Closet in 2014. My Sisters Closet's mission is to meet the needs of women through professional services and monthly workshop sessions.

Maria quickly realized that My Sisters Closet was just the beginning of what was to come. In 2016, God gave her the vision to launch My Sister CEO, a community of pioneering women who share the belief that with the support of one another their dreams can become a reality. My Sister CEO's mission is to foster collaboration and growth among women in their personal, business, and work life, through mentorship, coaching and community engagement.

Maria is a sought after speaker for delivering an empowering message as a panelist, breakout, and keynote speaker on topics such as Professional Development, Workforce Readiness and Executive Level Career Success Strategies, for a host of conferences, corporations, churches, organizations, and radio shows just to name a few. In 2017, Maria was chosen as the Career Coach for the Steve Harvey *Act Like A Success Conference* where she was a panelist and breakout speaker.

Maria has been profiled in a number of media platforms: The Washington Lawyer *DC Bar Magazine* and *The Washington Business Journal* for her article entitled; "Changing Dress Codes for law firms" and an interview entitled: "Change at the Top: A Two Part Series About Making The Most of Management Changes" where she discussed her successful integration and communication tactics and was featured as Working Mother of the Year in Working Mother Magazine.

Maria holds a top ranking position as Director of Administration for an international Law Firm, in addition to running two successful businesses. Her incredible story of determination and professional tenacity is nothing shy of amazing as Maria shares her story of how she worked her way to the top in her book "From The Front Desk To The Corner Office."

Maria cherishes her loving husband, her beautiful three daughters and her granddaughter the princess.

MY Sister CEO

When I look in the mirror I do not see myself looking back at me. I see the countless women who have inspired, motivated, challenged, mentored, and coached me. Without their guidance, my success would be non-existent and there would be no story to tell. Every time I take the stage to speak or walk into a meeting, I stand on the shoulders of the many women who have paved the way. They are the inspiration for me boldly speaking and walking tall.

My passion to carry the torch led to the birth of My Sisters Closet in 2014. Within three years we achieved more than 1,500 sponsors, members and supporters combined. We have partnered with local shelters and organizations that share our mission of meeting the needs of women, through professional development services, job-services, and related housing needs due to domestic incidents and more. The organization hosts monthly events such as Community Day, Annual Closet Swap, and Donation Day. We also host monthly workshop sessions to provide resources, social networking and strategic planning through resume building workshops, job fairs, and forums.

After years of working with women, I quickly realized that My Sisters Closet was just the beginning of what was to come. In 2016, God gave me the vision to launch My Sister CEO, a community of pioneering women who share the belief that with the support of one another our dreams can become a reality. The My Sister CEO mission is to foster collaboration and growth among women.

My Sister CEO, is an innovative network of women who have bonded together with the mission to learn success strategies and techniques that will lead to achievement within their lives, career and business. Our programs foster a model of mentoring, partnerships and networking. With these assets the women gain impactful techniques they can utilize to ignite their strengths, embrace their uniqueness, create opportunities, increase confidence, while pursuing their purpose. Our motto is; *Fear should not keep you from living your best life ever*! My Sister CEO movement is just getting started and we are looking forward to impacting women globally.

Stay connected to the movement…

Website: www.mysisterceo.com
Email maria@mysisterceo.com
Facebook: Maria Stanfield
Instagram: @mysisterceo
Twitter: MSCLOSET1

Made in the USA
Middletown, DE
25 April 2019